The
Bare
Truth

The Bare Truth:

101 Things Strippers Wish Men Would Learn

Pedro Miguel Arce

www.pedromiguelarce.com
pedro@pmarce.com

Cover Design: Arce Communications
Book Layout: P.M. Arce

For my mother:
> A strong independant woman
>> who taught me to love and respect.

And...
> All the strong women who have blessed my life since.

Acknowledgements

A special thank you to all the ladies who took the time to answer my questions. You are all beautiful in my eyes. It was a pleasure to have worked with you, partied with you, and learned from you.

A warm thanks to the all the security staff I've worked with in the past. Thank you for keeping me alive and out of too much trouble. It was an honor to have worked along side you my friends.

It was fun.

I raise my glass to you and wish you…

Salud, Dinero y Amor.
(health, money and love)

Introduction

The thing about being a working actor is that, more often than not, you have to work. My decision to become an actor went hand in hand with my decision to become a doorman. I wanted to have my days free to audition and have a job flexible enough to take time off to be on set. This road led me to a couple of strip clubs where I spent on and off almost eight years of my life.

I have met some of the sexiest, most desirable women around. I watched them work the floor, some with more ease than others, but all sexy and beautiful in their own ways. I watched the guys who paid hundreds and sometimes thousands of dollars for their time and company.

One night I asked my self, "what do these women want?" Men want them, but what is it that they want in a man.

So I asked them .

I asked over a hundred dancers, "What is the one thing you wish men would know?" I was amazed and grateful that they were so free to tell me. It was like they had been waiting to be asked that question for a long time. The following pages are filled with the top 101 answers they gave me.

Enjoy and learn. I did.

Pedro

1

"Be a gentleman.

It doesn't matter what the other person does as long as you're a gentleman."

Chase

2

"Be loyal."

Angel

3

"Be open and don't keep things inside, that goes for everything: wives, work, girlfriends... everything."

Lita

4

"Don't be cocky; don't act as if you're better than anyone. Let me see your wife."

Reba

5

"Don't treat women like objects."

Christy

6

"Shave your balls, keep it clean.

You expect us to stay clean and shaven,
so if you want to get more head…
do the same."

Fantasia

7

"Be true to yourself and others and in return they'll be true to you.

Be a real man"

Silver

8

"Men don't have to be good-looking as long as they're funny."

Dana

9

"Keep your mouth shut
or tell her what she wants to hear…
until you get some ass."

Montana

10

"Have some confidence."

Ava

11

"Be patient."

Bo

12

"When dealing with a woman remember that we think you are more complicated than you really are. Talk to women like they are four years old."

Rocki

13

"Shave your legs and back. It's disgusting
to be with a guy that has hair all over."

Malibu

14

"Be nice and polite. I like *Nice* People."

Danni

15

"Don't be an asshole and
learn to eat pussy."

Peaches

16

"Be positive."

Silky

17

"You know how girls like bad guys,
it wears off.

Be a nice guy and finish last."

Daisy

18

"Don't suck so hard on nipples,
just because *you* don't feel anything."

Destiny

19

"Be yourself, don't put up an act."

Sonia

20

"Don't try to control me."

Tyler

21

"When you're fucking don't be a rabbit
and just move in and out.

If you're going to move then move."

Whisper

22

"Think before you speak."

Ferrari

23

"Watch your wallet and
know where your heart is."

Lace

24

"Be patient and nice."

Zoey

25

"Don't let yourself be taken advantage of."

Harmony

26

"Put out more and be aggressive.
My whole life I've been told that men want
only one thing, you know what that is;
a mommy. Not sex, a mommy."

Cuddles

27

"Have self respect."

Kitty

28

"Be loyal
and cherish the one you're with."

Lacy

29

"When you're going down on a woman don't try to suck out an ovary."

Petal

30

"When meeting a girl for the first time don't offer to take her out for anything until you know her name."

Jinx

31

"Don't make everything about sex,
be patient and you'll get it."

Fire

32

"Always think before you act."

Ophelia

33

"Nipples are not radio dials."

Eden

34

"Never show off in front of a woman;
let her find out for herself."

Godiva

35

"Don't speak unless you're spoken to."

Krista

36

"Stop thinking that guns can solve shit."

Cookie

37

"Foreplay is paramount."

Dawn

38

"Keep opening doors."

Jordan

39

"Say what's on your mind."

Heaven

40

"Be my buddy. A man should have his girl's back even when she's wrong.

That's what a friend would do."

Baby

41

"Don't be so attached to your mother."

Fallon

42

"Ask, listen and do."

Leah

43

"Don't cheat.

Keep your dick in your pants and give me
your money."

Mink

44

"Keep your hands to yourself.
When you're at a club don't just grab a
girl's hand and start talking to her."

Lesha

45

"Give massages on a regular basis .
To get the pussy really really wet give her
little kisses as you massage her."

Midnight

46

"If you're putting a coat on a woman the ticket is to move the hair out of the way."

Fire

47

"Be respectful and honest."

Alabama

48

"If you find the right woman pay attention
to your her."

Honey

49

"Just because a girl dresses provocatively doesn't make her a slut."

Jamie

50

"Personal hygiene is important."

Nina

51

"Women like to be pursued."

Lexie

52

"Be more affectionate, guys are scared of showing their true feelings."

Ariel

53

"Love everyone and be appreciative. That way men wouldn't be so violent."

April

54

"Don't just love your woman respect her.
Love hurts, respect doesn't."

River

55

"No matter how strong a woman is,
she is still a fragile flower that
needs to be nurtured."

Harley

56

"Be confident, not cocky."

Nicole

57

"Take your time and be gentle."

Lainie

58

"Throw away all video games."

Sable

59

"Never say no to sex, because your neighbor might get it instead."

Tammi

60

"Don't make a woman your whole life."

Ember

61

"Be more romantic."

Leather

62

"Listen. One thing is to hear
and another is to listen."

Cinnamon

63

"When going down on a woman just know where to put your tongue. Put it on the clit and know how to work it."

Luscious

64

"Be real and upfront when breaking up with a woman.

Don't play head games."

Karma

65

"Don't look elsewhere when you have found something good."

Buffy

66

"Be honest to your self and you'll be honest to everyone else."

Robyn

67

"It's not all about looks,
personality plays."

Kayra

68

"Don't ever let a woman
be the source of your negativity."

Rita

69

"Always lick my pussy."

Willow

70

"Never lie."

Aries

71

"Put a sock in it and
quit while you're ahead."

Yvette

72

"A woman is a woman is a woman is a woman, take care of her."

Alison

73

"Don't get drunk."

Pixie

74

"Women need closure."

Emily

75

"Choose to be happy."

Melinda

76

"Treat your woman right and
pay attention to her."

Pisces

77

"Be nice, but not too nice."

Belinda

78

"Think with your head not your dick."

Eve

79

"Grow up!
Most guys are boys in men's bodies."

Damien

80

"Pay attention to everything a woman says after the word '*I*'."

Bianca

81

"It doesn't hurt to be nice."

Dixie

82

"Tell the woman you love
that you love her."

Wendy

83

"Sex: Keep it fun or you're done."

Red

84

"Cultivate a sense of humor, it helps."

Phoenix

85

"Respect and Honesty.
Honesty comes easily with respect."

Helena

86

"Learn the difference between your instinct, your head and your dick."

Venus

87

"Know what you're doing when you're down 'THERE'."

Coco

88

"Make me smile."

Diana

89

"Be true to yourself and be kind to others."

Licorice

90

"Licking is the way to the heart."

Martini

91

"Be like 'you', a teddy bear."

Serenity

92

"Don't forget to stay romantic
after you get the girl."

Snow

93

"A little innocent lie to cover some little innocent stuff keeps the relationship exciting."

Blondie

94

"Open up."

Roma

95

"Don't be cheap."

Mercedes

96

"I can't read your mind, tell me.
Be open with me."

Diamond

97

"Don't be a bitch."

Pandora

98

"Be the best you can be,
improve your life all around."

Bubbles

99

"Don't use other people's brains
as your mirror."

Candice

100

"Think it over 100 times before saying anything to a woman."

Hope

101

"All you need to know about women is
that we want what we want,
when we want it, but most of the time...
we don't know what that is."

Muse

www.ingramcontent.com/pod-product-compliance
Lightning Source LLC
Chambersburg PA
CBHW081215020426

42331CB00012B/3031